SPUNKY SCIENCE

CAN:

✓ Make copies for your students for educational use

✓ Print content in different forms such as a booklet

✓ Print in various sizes to fit your needs

✓ Post content on a school-based platform for student use or reference

CAN'T:

✗ Distribute digital or copies to others without an additional purchase

✗ Remove Spunky Science logo or copyright

✗ Resell or redistribute in any way other than originally intended by Spunky Science

SENSE RECEPTORS

Animals use their perceptions and memories to guide their actions.

A CATS WHISKERS ARE THEIR BUILT-IN RADAR SYSTEM.

Their whisker follicle is loaded with nerves while the tip is called the proprioceptor. Together, they are very good at sensing vibrations.

Bats sense the world around them by using ECHOLOCATION

LATERAL LINE
Detects movements and vibrations in the water.

Smell is 10,000x better than humans!

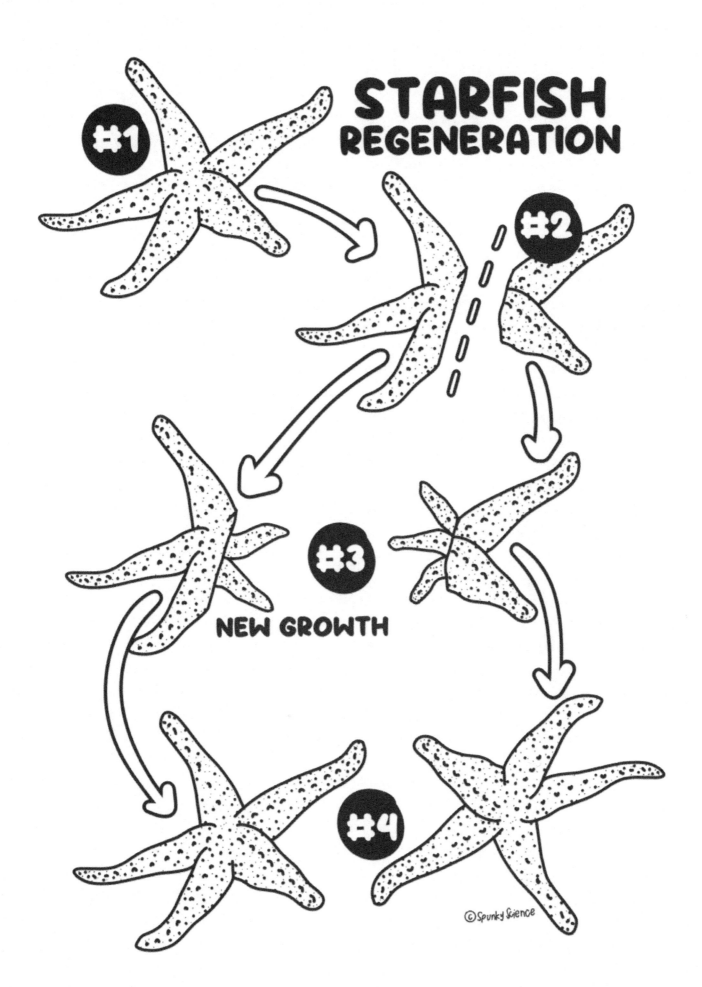

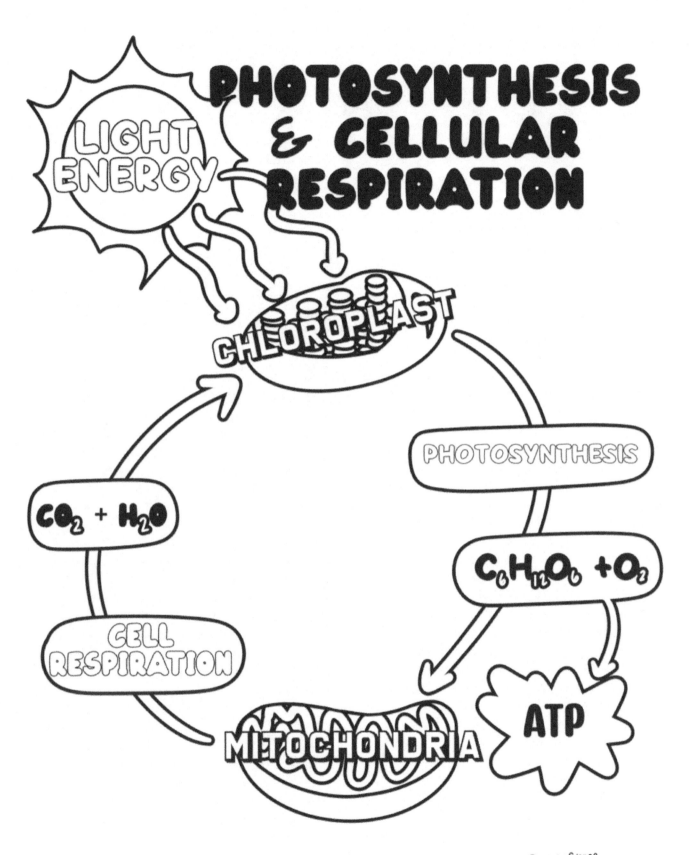

PHOTOSYNTHESIS & CELLULAR RESPIRATION

LIGHT ENERGY

CHLOROPLAST

PHOTOSYNTHESIS

$CO_2 + H_2O$

$C_6H_{12}O_6 + O_2$

CELL RESPIRATION

MITOCHONDRIA

ATP

©Spunky Science

CELLULAR RESPIRATION

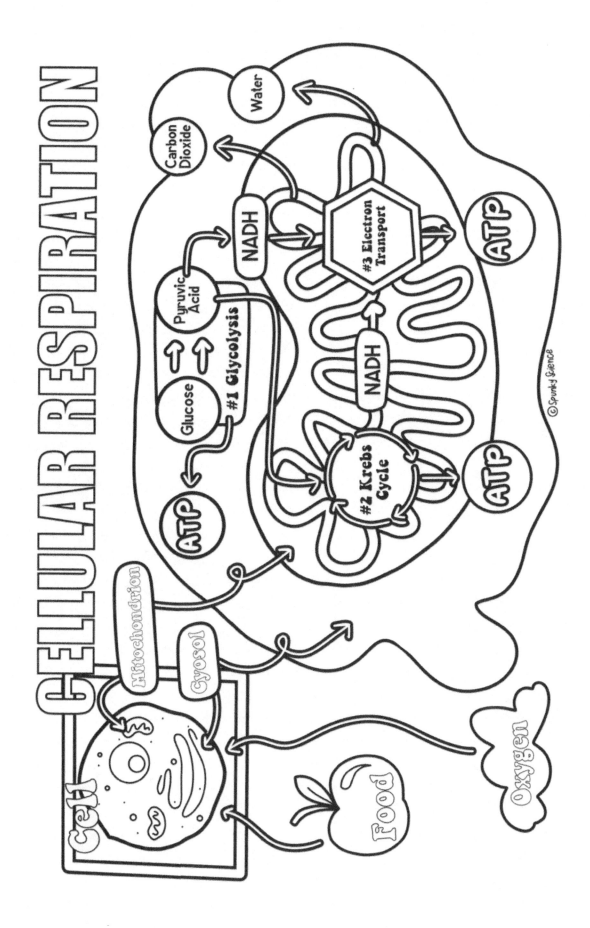

©Spunky Science

HOW CLOUDS ARE MADE

SUN

THE SUN HEATS UP WATER AND LAND SURFACES

COLD AIR MEETS WATER VAPOR CAUSING CONDENSATION TO OCCUR

WARM AIR AND WATER VAPOR RISES

water

sand

STEPS:

WATER VAPOR

DUST

WATER DROPS

CLOUD DROPLET

CLOUD

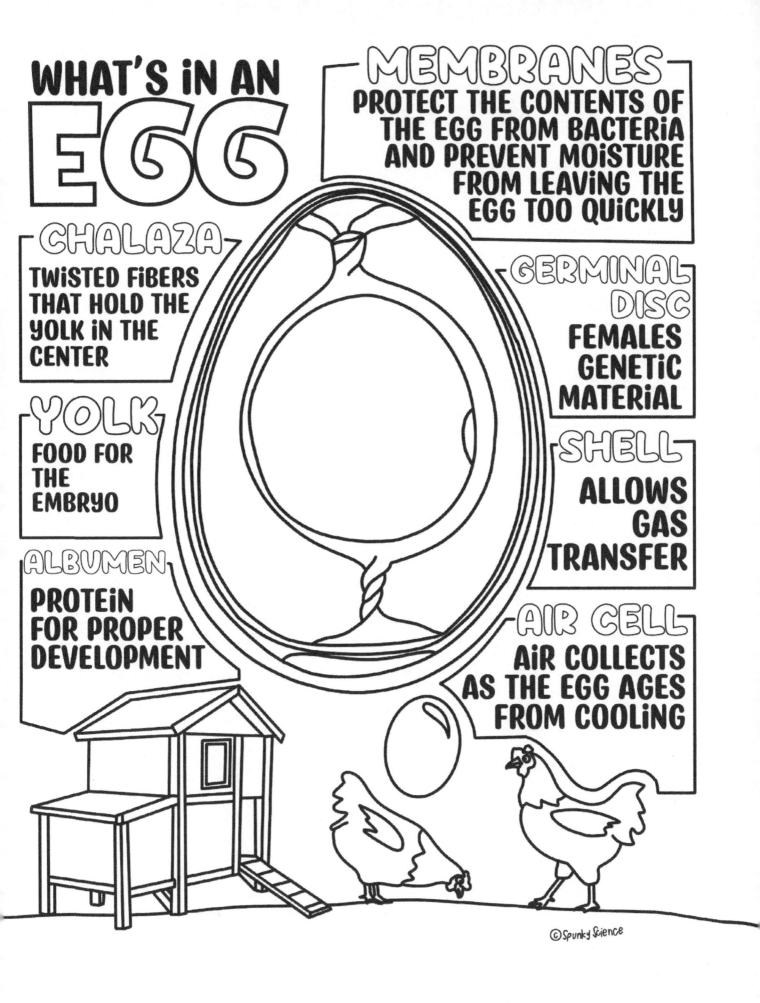

WHAT'S IN AN EGG

MEMBRANES
PROTECT THE CONTENTS OF THE EGG FROM BACTERIA AND PREVENT MOISTURE FROM LEAVING THE EGG TOO QUICKLY

CHALAZA
TWISTED FIBERS THAT HOLD THE YOLK IN THE CENTER

GERMINAL DISC
FEMALES GENETIC MATERIAL

YOLK
FOOD FOR THE EMBRYO

SHELL
ALLOWS GAS TRANSFER

ALBUMEN
PROTEIN FOR PROPER DEVELOPMENT

AIR CELL
AIR COLLECTS AS THE EGG AGES FROM COOLING

© Spunky Science

BUTTERFLY LIFE CYCLE

EGG

ADULT

(CATERPILLAR) LARVA

EMERGING ADULT

(PUPA) CHRYSALIS

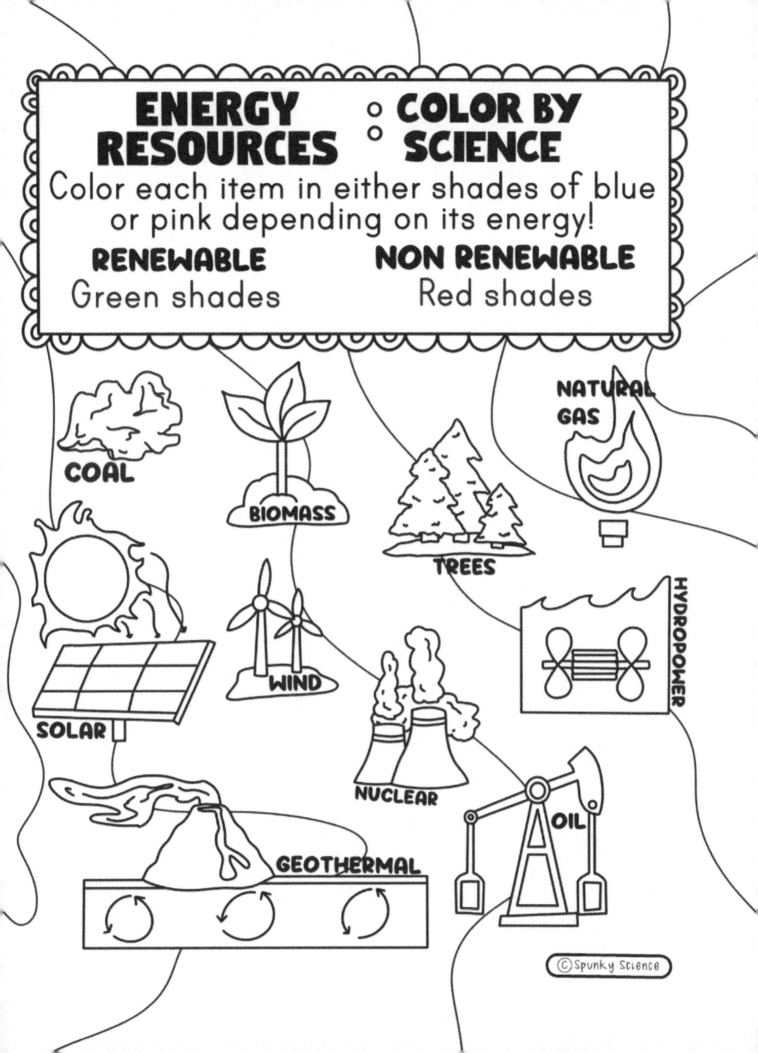

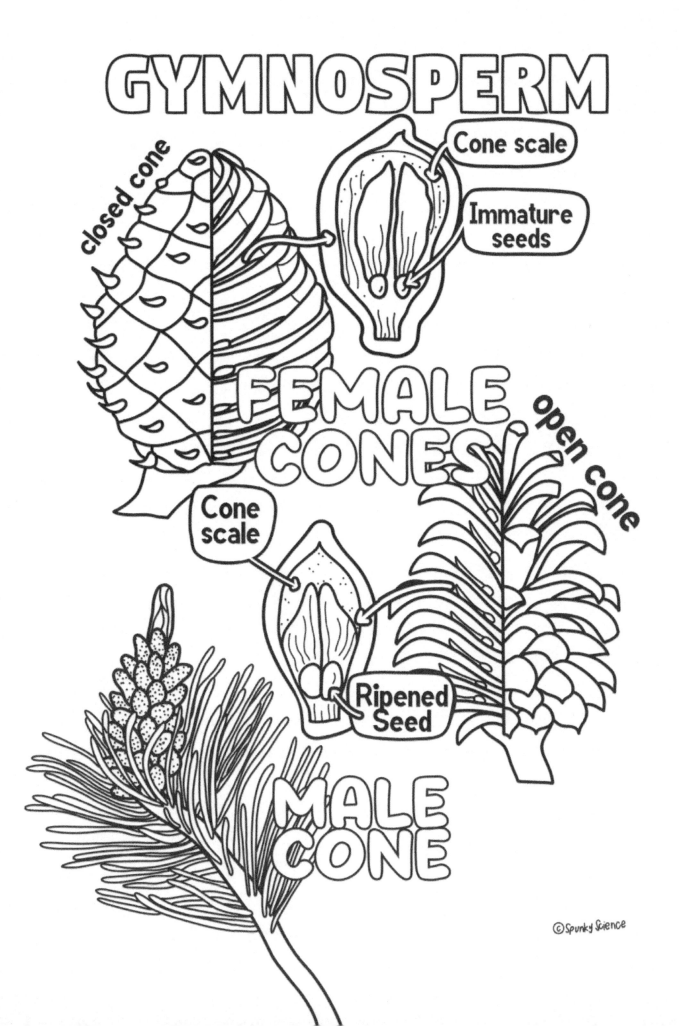

TARDIGRADES

Discovered in 1773

Capable of repairing their DNA after radiation damage.

Water Bears

Moss Piglets

Extremophiles

0.5mm-1mm in length

Can survive up to 10 days in space!

EYE ANATOMY

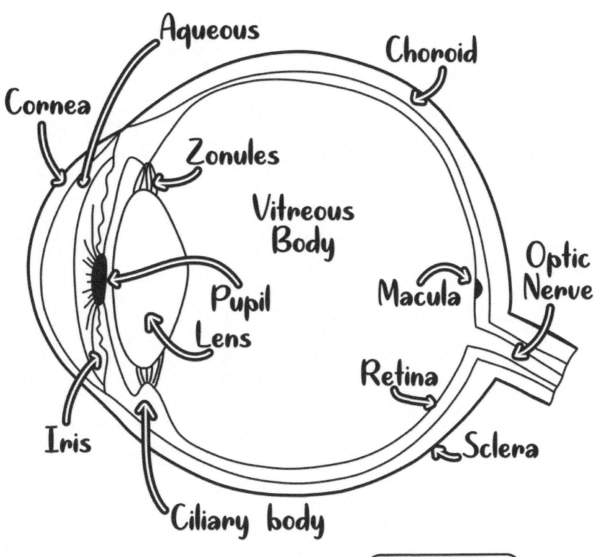

Aqueous
Choroid
Cornea
Zonules
Vitreous Body
Optic Nerve
Pupil
Lens
Macula
Iris
Retina
Sclera
Ciliary body

you are the BRIGHTEST person I've XENON this planet

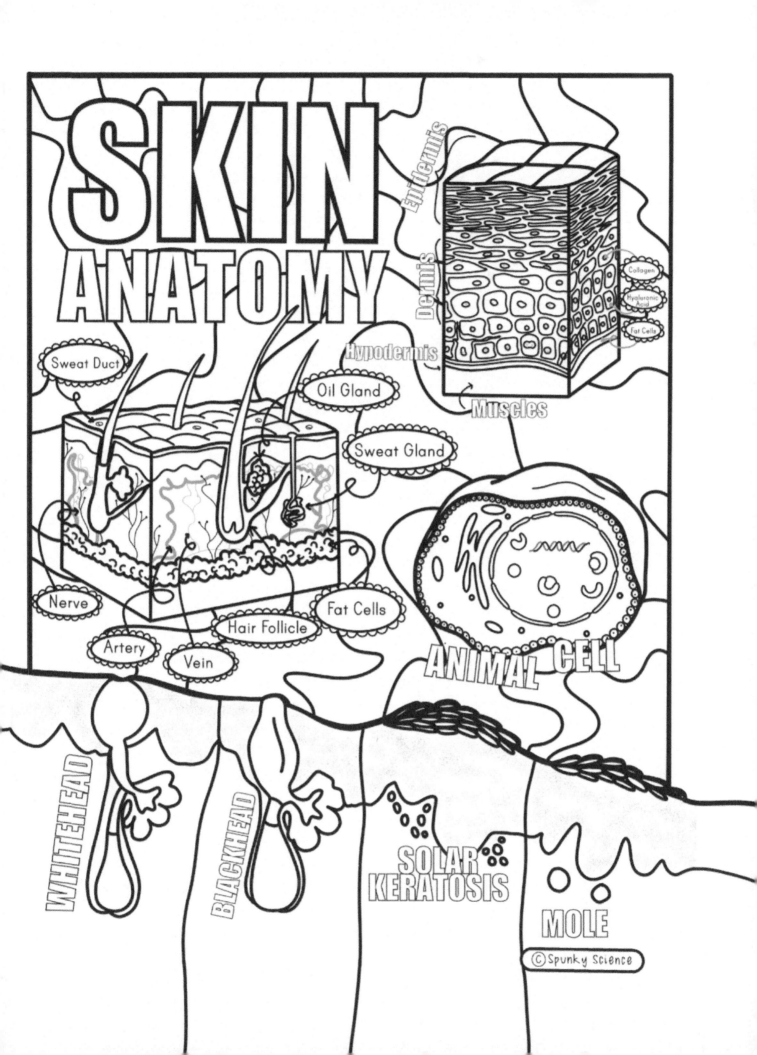

FORMATION OF SEDIMENTARY ROCK

#1 WEATHERING

Breaks down materials of the Earth's crust into smaller pieces through water, wind, ice, acids, and changes in temperature.

#2 EROSION

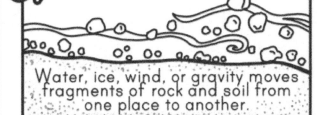

Water, ice, wind, or gravity moves fragments of rock and soil from one place to another.

#3 DEPOSITION

Sediments are dropped in specific locations.

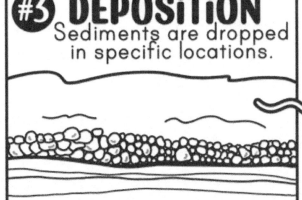

#4 COMPACTION

Sediments are pressed together from the above pressure of water and other sediment layers.

#5 CEMENTATION

Sediments are cemented together by natural cements such as clay or minerals.

LARGER SEDIMENTS

SMALLER GRAINS

#6

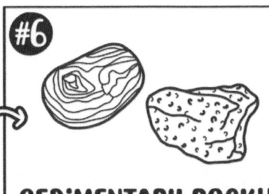

SEDIMENTARY ROCK!!

© Spunky Science

BLOB FISH
Scientific name:
Psychrolutes marcidus

Above the Surface

Lack a swim bladder

Diet: They do not hunt, they wait patiently for their food to come and then they consume it. Diet includes slugs, sea urchins, and snails.

Blobfish look like normal fish at their normal depths of 2,000-4,000 feet under the surface.

3,700ft below surface

BASKING SHARK
Scientific name: Cetorhinus maximus

Not aggressive and are harmless to humans.

second largest fish in the world 🌎

swim with their mouths open to filter the plankton out of the water for food.

Grow up to 45ft and 10,000Lbs

CELL ORGANELLES

CYTOPLASM
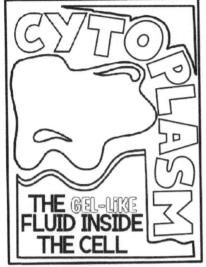
THE GEL-LIKE FLUID INSIDE THE CELL

Endoplasmic RETICULUM

PRODUCES PROTEINS

CENTRAL VACUOLE
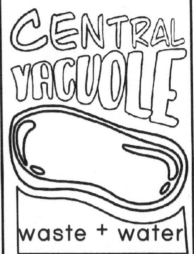
waste + water

CHLOROPLAST

Convert light into usable energy

RIBOSOME
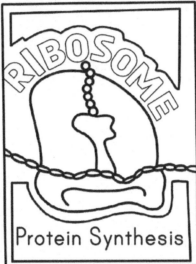
Protein Synthesis

GENERATES ATP
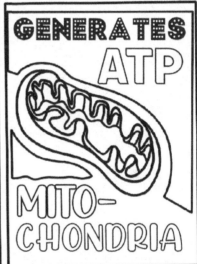
MITO-CHONDRIA

NUCLEUS

STORE DNA   CONTROL CENTER

PROVIDES STRENGTH & PROTECTION

CELL WALL

GOLGI APPARATUS

CELLS POST OFFICE   PACKAGES PROTEINS

© Spunky Science

MICROBIOLOGIST

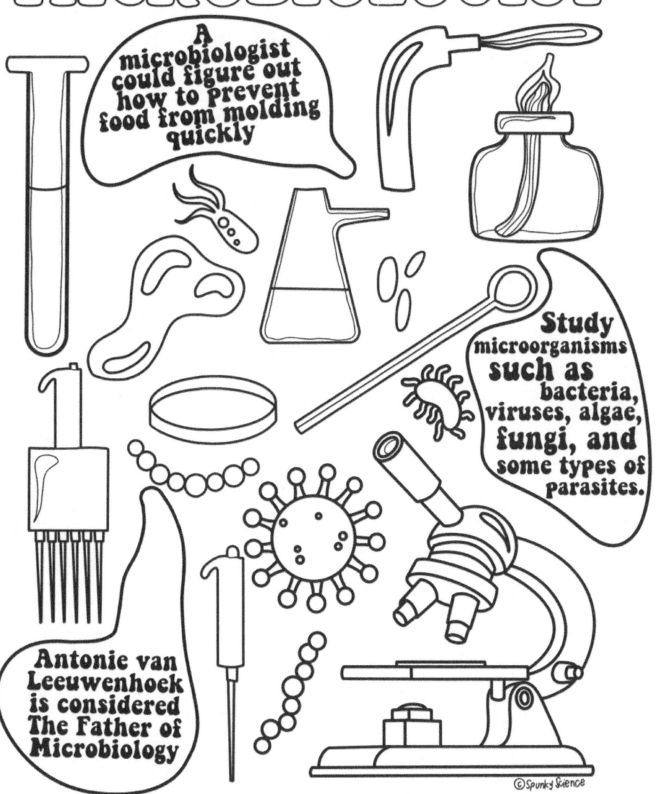

A microbiologist could figure out how to prevent food from molding quickly

Study microorganisms **such as** bacteria, viruses, algae, **fungi, and** some types of parasites.

Antonie van Leeuwenhoek is considered The Father of Microbiology

©Spunky Science

4 TYPES OF TISSUES
IN THE HUMAN BODY

CONNECTIVE

Tissue that connects, supports, binds, or separates other tissues or organs.

EPITHELIAL

Tissue that forms the covering on all internal and external organs. They serve as a protective barrier as well as secreting and absorbing substances.

MUSCLE

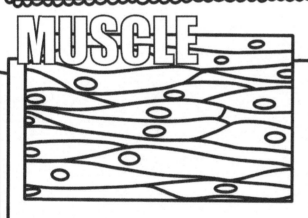

Tissue that attach to bones or internal organs and blood vessels and are responsible for movement.

NERVOUS

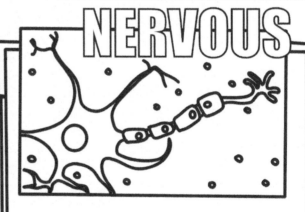

Tissues that are the main component of the nervous system-made of primarily neurons and glial cells.

CHEMICAL REACTIONS

When two or more different substances
are mixed, a new substance is formed.

Odor produced

Color change

Temperature change

A Solid is formed

Precipitate

Gas created

VINEGAR AND
BAKING SODA
ARE A
CHEMICAL
REACTION

vinegar

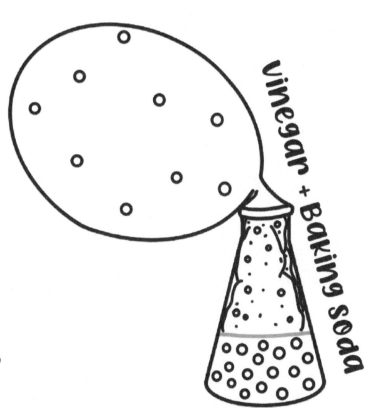

vinegar + Baking soda

A new substance is created, but
mass is not created nor destroyed.

SATURN

SATURN GIVES OFF MORE ENERGY THAN IT RECEIVES FROM THE SUN

HAS THOUSANDS OF RINGS MADE OF ICE AND ROCK

SATURN HAS THE FASTEST WINDS OF ANY OTHER PLANET AT 1,100MPH!

SATURN HAS 53 KNOWN MOONS WITH AN ADDITIONAL 29 MOONS AWAITING CONFIRMATION.

SATURN IS ONE OF FIVE PLANETS ABLE TO BE SEEN WITH THE NAKED EYE.

DWARF PLANETS

AND THEIR MOONS

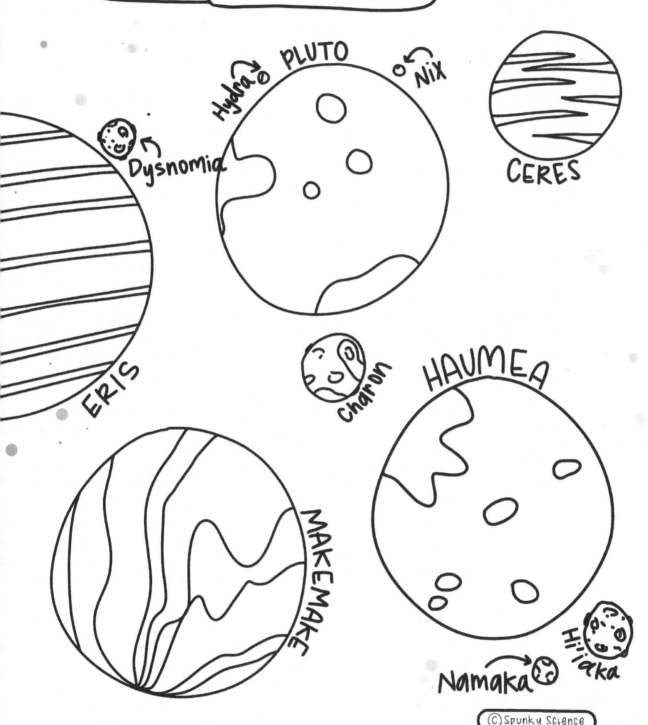

ERIS

Dysnomia

Hydra

PLUTO

Nix

CERES

Charon

HAUMEA

MAKEMAKE

Namaka

Hi'iaka

© Spunky Science

LAYERS OF SOIL

HUMUS	Contains living material, plants, decaying leaves and more.
TOPSOIL	The layer where most nutrients for plants are found.
SUBSOIL	Made up of sand, soil, silt, and clay.
PARENT MATERIAL	Made of mostly broken up rocks and some broken tree roots.
BEDROCK	This layer is composed of solid rock and is below all other layers of soil.

PERIODIC TABLE

Atomic Number

Symbol

Name

Atomic Weight

N 7
Nitrogen
14.0067

Each box on the periodic table represents a specific element. Its location on the PT was carefully determined based on each elements physical and chemical properties. These trends make it easy to remember the common properties of elements!

Color code each group of elements!

Alkali metals	Rare Earth
Alkali Earth metals	Halogens
Transition metals	Noble Gases
Other metals	Actinide Elements
Other Non metals	

Color code periods and family

Each horizontal row is called a period while each vertical column is called a group or family. As you increase the atomic number, you **gain** one proton and one electron.

PLANTCELL

Plant cells are the basic unit of life in the kingdom plantae. They are eukaryotic cells, which have a true nucleus along with specialized structures called organelles that carry out different functions.

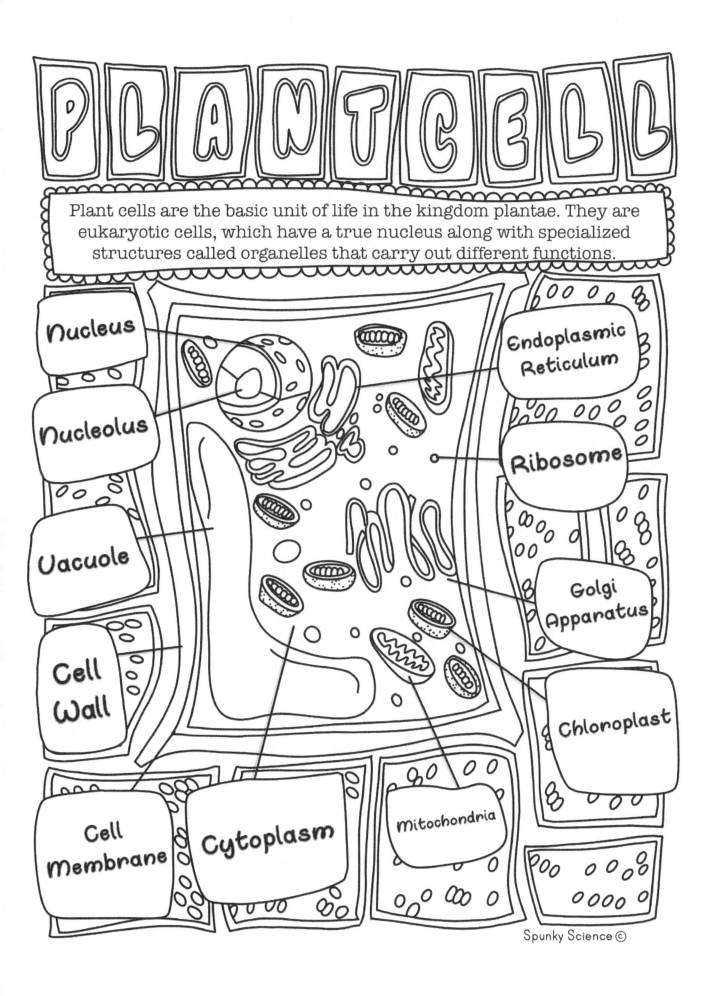

Nucleus

Nucleolus

Vacuole

Cell Wall

Cell Membrane

Cytoplasm

Mitochondria

Endoplasmic Reticulum

Ribosome

Golgi Apparatus

Chloroplast

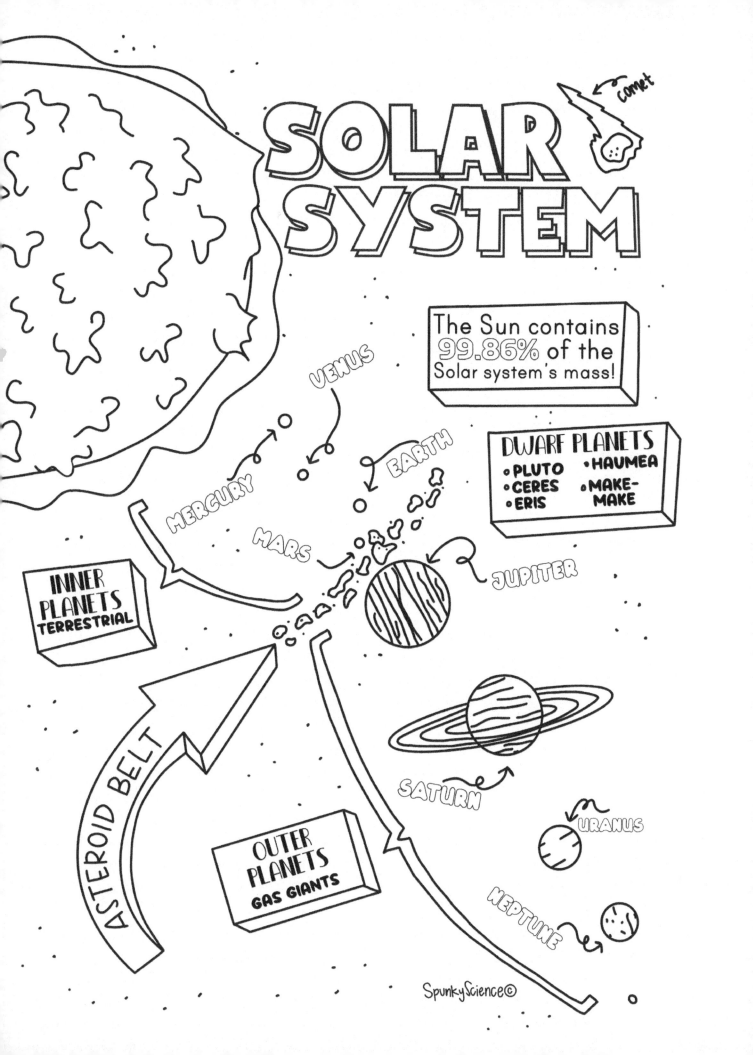

WHAT IS DENSITY?

length
width
height

THE AMOUNT OF PARTICLES PER GIVEN SPACE

SAME NO MATTER HOW BIG OR SMALL

IDENTIFIES UNKNOWN SUBSTANCES

REGULAR SHAPED OBJECTS CAN BE EASILY MEASURED WITH A RULER

IRREGULAR SHAPED OBJECTS

GRADUATED CYLINDER MEASURES VOLUME OF IRREGULAR SHAPED OBJECTS

$$D = \frac{MASS}{VOLUME}$$

SpunkyScience©

ELEMENTS

Periodic table of elements

Atomic number →

80   200.59

Hg

MERCURY

← Atomic weight

→ Symbol

→ Name

Hint! ONLY ONE CAPITAL LETTER

Water molecule

H_2O

H   O   H

One type of atom

C or C C

ONE CARBON ATOM= C
TWO CARBON ATOMS= C_2

Made of two or more different kinds of atoms chemically combined.

BOHR MODEL SHOWING CARBON

Represented by a chemical formula

$C_{12} H_{22} O_{11}$ (sugar)

Made from different kinds of atoms.

Subscripts identify the number of atoms.

one kind of atom

BUILDING BLOCK

Made of one or more of the same type of atom.

Spunky Science ©

H   F

← HF

COMPOUNDS

SpunkyScience©

ocean Layers

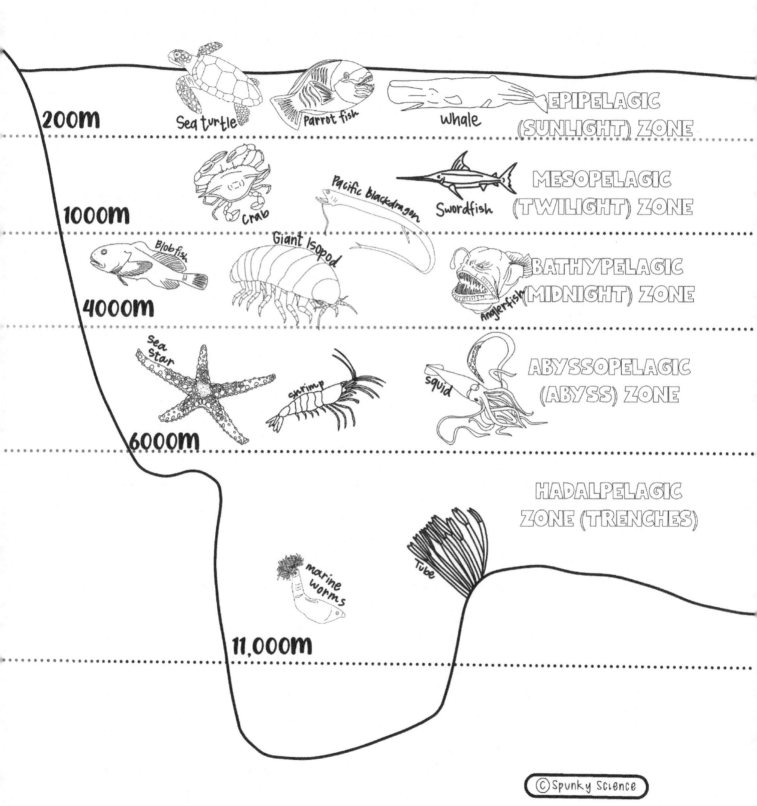

200m — Sea turtle, parrot fish, whale — EPIPELAGIC (SUNLIGHT) ZONE

1000m — crab, Pacific blackdragon, Swordfish — MESOPELAGIC (TWILIGHT) ZONE

4000m — Blob fish, Giant Isopod, Anglerfish — BATHYPELAGIC (MIDNIGHT) ZONE

6000m — Sea Star, shrimp, squid — ABYSSOPELAGIC (ABYSS) ZONE

11,000m — marine worms, Tube — HADALPELAGIC ZONE (TRENCHES)

© Spunky Science

Cross-Pollination

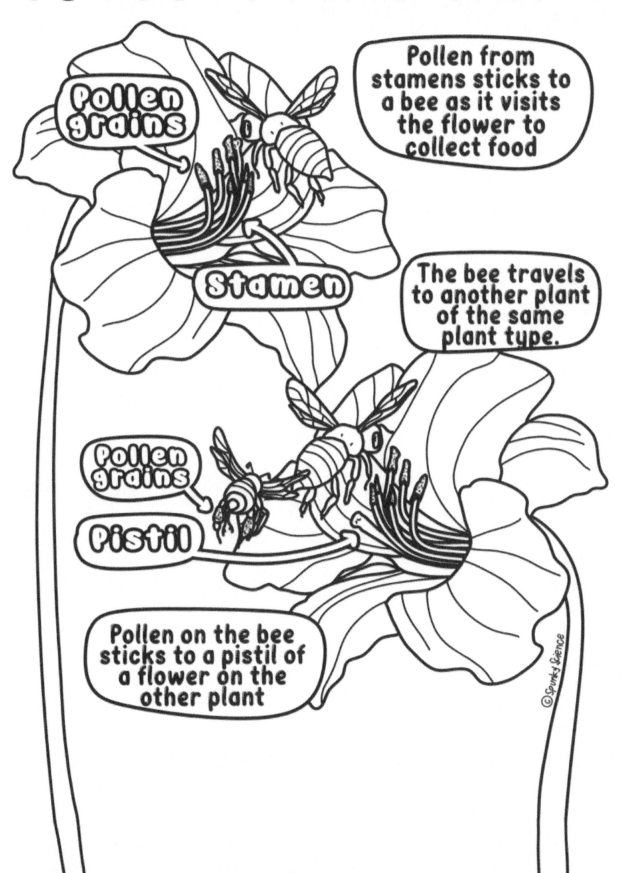

CARING FOR A
BETTA FISH

With care, Betta fish can live as 5 years!

Water temperature sure be between 75-80 degrees F.

Aquarium size per Betta should be about 5 Gallons.

In a home aquarium, Beta fish eat betta pellets, bloodworms, brine shrimp, daphnia, mysis shrimp, tubifex worms, and mosquito larvae.

©Spunky Science

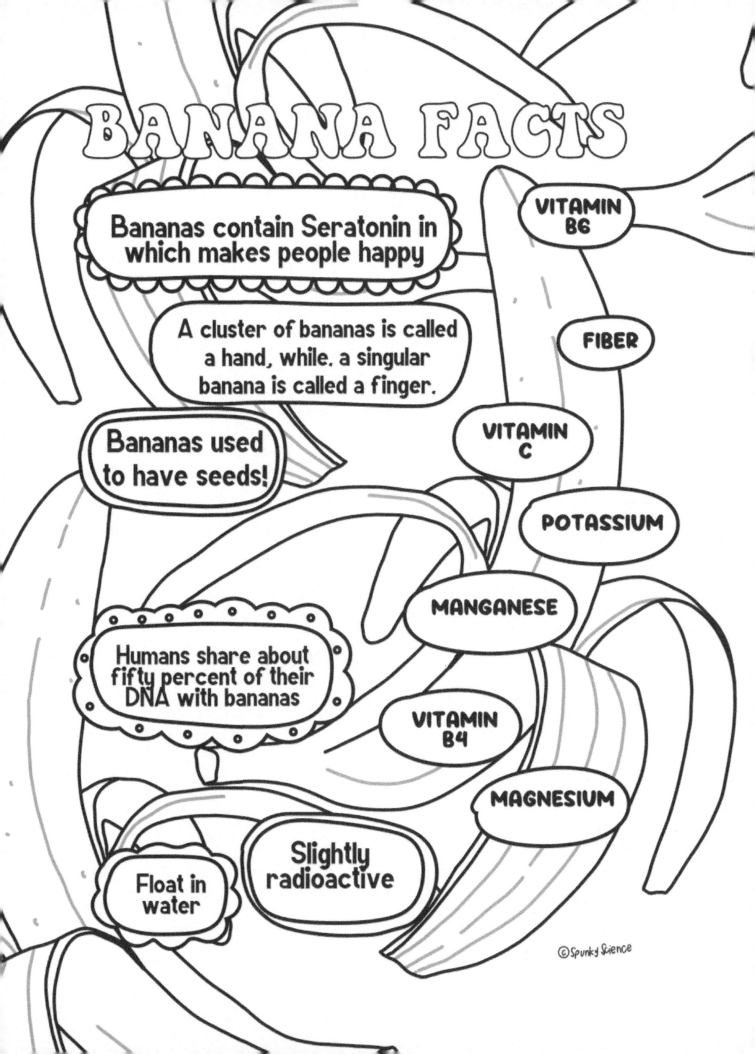

CYCLE OF A
DUNG BEETLE

ADULTS ARE ATTRACTED TO FRESH SMELLING DUNG

ROLLERS REMOVE A BALL OF DUNG AND ROLL IT TO A TUNNEL

ADULT EMERGES FROM THE DUNG BALL AND LEAVES THE TUNNEL

FEMALE LAYS AN EGG IN DUNG BALL

LARVA PUPATES IN THE DUNG BALL

LARVA EATS AND GROWS IN THE DUNG BALL

©Spunky Science

89835813R00046